STORIES
OF OUR LIFE

SALMEEN AL HATHRASH

INDIA • SINGAPORE • MALAYSIA

ISBN 979-8-88704-326-5

ACKNOWLEDGMENT

"I'd like to thank Notion press for helping me publish this book and Mr. Barath Raj Muthukumar of notion press who has been of great help through the whole process, I'd also like to thank my friend Manuel Markley Carvalho who had me motivated me in getting this book published"

CONTENTS

MAZE

Burning eyes, beating heart,
Yes, I know that I'm alive,
just Like Alice in the wonderland I'm lost,
Riddle after riddle, call it maze of life,

LOVE LIFE

Too many love stories, too many loves lies,

Too many love categories, yes true with time love dies,

But I'm not here to tell that,

And rather not be the person that sits back and cries,

I'd prefer moving on with all the memories I hide.

UNFORGETTABLE MEMORIES

Sweeter than sugar, sour like lemon,
I thought we'd be lemonade,
But you let our love fade.
I thought it'll be from dusk till dawn,
Like Zayn Malik's song,
But all we did was go wrong.
I'd love to apologize,
But you were busy counting dollars,
While I was making wishes out of shooting stars.
You remember 11:11 and those wishes you made,
If you had made them from your heart, that would've been great.
Now until next time I bid farewell,
Crazy world it is a second ago we were at the sea saw,
Now I'm by the beach collecting seashell

CANDLE LOVE

Every day, every night,
Every left, every right,
For every thought of you in my life,
I shall burn a candle to remind,
The wax melts just like your love,
And I burn with the hope that I'll survive,
Hope that your love shall revive.

TILL THEN

Lost in space, lost the will but look at my face,
Lost the pace, but still, still in the chase,
Trying my best, trying to be the best,
I shall succeed, till then I shall not rest.

SURVIVE

A little bit of this, a little bit of that,
A little bit of everything, yes that's what I like,
But everything is what we can't have,
Neither a little from here, nor a little from there,
I now just thrive to survive,
On I.V brain dead, heart failed waiting to be revived.

WHEN EVER YOU MISS ME.

Agreed that we've walked away,

But know that,

Whenever you miss me, you know the way,

Never to forget each other,

Is what you used to say,

But know that,

Whenever you miss me, you know the way,

How much ever distance there be,

For you not to be in my view,

In my dreams is where I'll see you,

Let there be rain,

Whenever you miss me, you know the way.

MAYBE

To be or not to be,

May it be or not,

Does it even matter when your world comes crashing down?

Are we to be free,

Or not to be maybe,

Walking through memory lane buried deep in the ground.

CURTAIN CALL

It's the curtain call,
As the show gets over, we bow down,
Here comes the call, here the curtain falls,
The time slows over, feet shivering on.
Getting through time is like an act on a stage,
Fixing life, our lives page after page,
Just hoping to get through the day.

HEARTLESS

Darkness in my mind,
No light in my heart,
Coldest I've ever felt my blood is fighting back.

BED TIME THOUGHTS

I put my head down to bed
Stuck on this boat
Sailing through my thoughts
Through the flashback of all the wars I fought
A misery a memory
A moment maybe crazy
I just don't want to be in this place right now
Someone please tell me how

NO MATTER WHAT....

There was a girl that a guy fell in love with,

She always wondered the reason thinking she wasn't perfect,

The guy din bother weather she was perfect or not all he knew was she was worth it,

With time he liked her more,

Was it her attitude,

Or was it her charm,

All the guys knew he loved her for who she was that he was sure,

She put her trust she put in efforts,

To not let her down he did all he could,

This is not about anyone else but me and you.

ANOTHER CHANCE.

Word to word trying to get through all my thoughts,

You love me now, you'll hate me later,

You tell me let's be friends, how does it even matter,

There are things we got to sort out,

Look at me know I mean it,

There'll be a time when you'll feel like I had given all I had,

You'll know I was different,

That I wasn't bad nor was I crazy or mad,

Was this a mistake why do I regret,

Why did I let myself free up?

Why did I give it another chance?

– Salmeen Al Hathrash

DO YOU REMEMBER

Do you remember the good times?

The love the smiles,

Do you remember when we were happier,

When we worried less when it was simpler,

Do you remember the moments we had?

When we lived the good, fought through the bad,

What's happened now,

Drifting apart, what is it that I need to realise that I need to know,

The magic is fading the love is vanishing,

But I'm here remembering through,

Why did we talk it out?

And then say what was it about,

Why did we hold on, why did we carry on?

Why couldn't we be strong, just sorry on and on,

Why did this not last,

Why you had to tell me this won't go along.

– Salmeen Al Hathrash

HALFWAY THERE

Pour me a drink, its cold,

Emotions overflowing,

Flowing out growing old,

Making moves forgot to think twice,

Decisions now I wonder how where they not bold nor wise,

A million thoughts a lot to sort out,

Crying out loud,

For the sake of God understand,

You know what I'm talking about,

Blank from the head,

Trying to get back to bed,

Can't get things straight,

Thinking about people getting it through with meds,

A lot of words,

Words I know could hurt,

– Salmeen Hathrash

HER WISH

She wakes up every morning,

With hopes someone would love her more,

Love her back, give her the loving,

The loving she needs,

The love that's true and not those that just walk in and walk out when they are done with feelings,

She has lost the meaning of love,

With so much of lust around, she wants a man that could go down,

Tell her what she means, take her to the sky and be there at the ground,

That's not afraid to fight, choose her over the wrong and right,

Be there for her let it be day or Night,

Be her desire be her smile,

Be in her heart and her mind,

Be her strength be her knight,

Be her world her words,

Be what she wants,

Be the magic, the rabbit out of the hat,

Be the happiness,

Be the tissue that wipes the tear before it even drops down her eyes,

Be the one who brings faith and meaning of love back in her life,

Be the one who stands in front behind and even by her side,

So, it's him she sees at every sight.

A LOT BY THE LAST PAGE

There's a lot to see a lot to feel

I'd want to believe there's more to this world than what I breathe

There's a lot going on in my mind

But I want to believe the night too shines bright

No more emotions, got nothing

I'm trying to fight it, I'm always fighting

Bars everywhere locked in a cage,

Imprisoned by my own life

Hoping that my story ends

And its happy ending by the last page.

LOSE TO WIN.

A little sacrifice
For a greater gain
Lose for once
So, you can do better in the next chance
Let them feel you're wasting your time
But not know that you're climbing to be a prime
Let them feel it's all out of the line
But not know you've done through the mile
Sometimes it's better to let go
But sometimes just hold on let it flow
It may take time it may be a little slow
But when it comes, you'll not feel low
For now, there's a lot left to know
And a lot left to see and show
Theres a melody out in the meadow
Just open the window
And peek out the mind

Peek out and see what life has got to offer you

Negativity is there for a reason

But it's like the seasons

So, step on

And see on

Cause there's more than what's gone

– Salmeen Al Hathrash

SHE GAVE UP

Slow it down hold on,

Theres a lot to come now,

Sleepless nights you complain

He left walked away that's your thing

Crying over some small pain

Complaining he is off to be someone else's king

All along you complain you got nothing to gain

Trying to meditate

Smoking helps you elevate

Thinking it will help you levitate

Thoughts put side thinking it straight

Will he be back?

Life going off track

Songs after songs

Cuts body cracked

Its story of a girl who said bye for one last time

Took her life

Loving endlessly was her crime
She tried and tried held on tight
Each and every day through those dark nights
She laid on the floor
Blood all over laid dead with a smile
While he was away playing with someone else's life.

CURTAIN CALL

By the shore, listening to birds the waves,
Peace of mind, trying to leave everything behind,
Close the door, trying to get through the days,
Race of thoughts, things to get off but never mind,
Bright blue sky, bright blue sea,
Everyone at peace, peace to be,
Still lost with all the thoughts,
Where to go what to do, got lot to sort,
Been asleep throughout time, throughout life,
Trying to get through the hurt and recovering through words,
It's a dream in a dream in a dream,
Getaway rowing a boat through a stream.
Something don't make sense, curtain call,
Trying to see world through filter lens, curtains unfold,
End of the show end of success, curtain falls,

– Salmeen Hathrash

HOPES OF A MIRACLE

Everyone is leaving, most are cheating,

Here I am grazing, looking through the sky,

With hopes of one day, a miracle might come my way.

Times flying, here I am crying,

Trying to survive this life,

There's lot to speak lot to say,

But I still keep quite with a hope a miracle might come my way.

In this world so cruel,

The world that uses people as fuel,

Here I stay with hopes someday a miracle might come my way.

– Salmeen Al Hathrash

BLACKS AND WHITES

Blacks and whites
All these bright lights who knew they shine
All the blues and yellows
And all those colour that contrast
Who knew it would be you.
It was never to be, I wished to walk away
It was never the intention to stay
I wish to step back
Close my eyes and avoid all the colours
Avoid the thoughts of you in my mind
Try to live life through the dark side
Cause out of all the colours
White and black have been the best of opposite
Now darkness with a little light is part of my life

– Salmeen Al Hathrash

DON'T YOU KNOW OF HIS THOUGHTS

"Don't you look me in the eye

Don't you try to dig what's in my heart

Don't get in my head

Don't try to know my past

Let me be, let me live

Don't you know it's hard for me to survive?

It's easy to judge you won't realise

Realise what it's like to put on a smile

Wake up every morning

Don't you know how hard it is

Moving around smile

Don't you know

What do you know about the things I've been through?

What do you know?

What do you know"?

This is what runs his mind every time someone pricks the smile in his life

This is what he wants to say every time someone spoils his day

This is what he feels like every time a bad thing strikes

This is what he hides

This is what he hides

– Salmeen Al Hathrash

ACROSS THE SEA I'D BE

Across the ocean the sea
I'll be there when you'll need me
Lost a lot but I'd still fight for it
All this time I was stupid I was crazy
Even after all of this and that
When you need, I'd be.
Cause there's nothing in this world I couldn't beat
I'd run miles swim across the Nile
Even after what you've done, I'd still be by your side
I know what it feels to frown, never want to see you cry

– Salmeen Al Hathrash

DON'T LOSE HOPE

I live to the rhythm,

Live it from my mind,

I don't go on by the system.

Get up change, there's enough time,

Run on the plane hasn't taken off,

Find the meaning, find the reason,

Push on you know you are strong,

Go on like yourself more than you could love someone else,

Go on spend some time put on a smile,

You know better there's nothing you can't do,

Why hold yourself back, go on be you,

There's a lot but never lose hope.

– Salmeen Al Hathrash

FAITH, BELIEVE AND HOPE

What are we here for,

Why do we look at our downfall?

What are we here we aren't at all sure,

Why do we see as it's always rainfall?

We wish for more, more and more,

We forgot that we learn to run after we learn to walk and walk after we've learned to crawl.

Why are we always bothered?

Lost in thoughts, what shall we do,

All the pain we carry forward,

But always forget it's the choices made by you.

Let us stop and think,

Hope on hope we make it through,

Bother less smile often,

Our joyful moments might be few,

But forget those moment make us weakly stronger.

Believe in what?

Believe in ourselves,

Believe we can make it,

We hope to believe and believe to hope,

That's faith and that pushes us further ahead.

We must have faith in our believes and keep our hopes high,

We might fall,

But we get up cause sky is no more the limit,

Let your wings out and fly.

– Salmeen Al Hathrash

REASONS TO LIVE

The blue sky, the green lands,
The tall trees, the flowing water,
The blowing wind, the warm sand.
There is lot to see in this world,
The strong standing mountains,
Falling off a cliff,
Diving down splashing through the sea,
The intense feels.
There is a lot to do in this world,
We make mistakes we frown over it,
There is no reason to live through it,
Go on the world holds a lot,
What are you worrying about?
There is magic around you,
There is a lot to do,
There is soul within you,
Don't frown over mistakes that are few.

Walk in talk out,

Don't think you lack thoughts.

There are fights,

Sometimes they are right,

Sometimes wrong,

If you lose, don't you think you aren't strong.

There is a lot to smile for.

WHAT POETRY IS

Poetry is feelings,
Feelings that I feel,
Poetry is emotions,
Emotions that make my life,
Poetry is words lines sentences,
Which describe us the best,
Poetry is a way to live,
Poetry is my get away,
Poetry is the frown the smile,
Poetry is the little stars at night,
Poetry is thoughts,
Thoughts put in words,
Poetry is the footsteps we take daily.

– Salmeen Al Hathrash

LIFE IS A GAME

Growing up stages after stages,
Levelling up,
Life is a game,
Skills and rewards, if we tend to fail,
Repeat.
When things get hard,
We usually need a break,
Pause and take time off,
Cause there Is a lot coming through.
Not everything is planned to go along,
Sometimes there are paths that's not decided,
Don't lose hope, do something wrong,
You are strong.
Life is a game just play conquer be a legend.
It's not the same as everybody else,
So don't go on trying to compare,
Your end is different.

– Salmeen Al Hathrash

BY YOURSELF

There is a lot to learn,

The past is to burn,

Life isn't easy, pretty many twists and turn,

There is a fight to be won,

It's you alone, and none.

– Salmeen Al Hathrash

LIFE'S OFFER

Lot of words to choose from,

Feeling weak but trying to stay firm,

Hopes drown down in bottles of rum,

Hmmm, it's been long enough now you start to feel numb,

Holding on a little longer wishing someone might come,

Feeling dumb bashing through music trying to think everything around is just drums,

Thought this would last long, long term,

Turning towards smokes chain smoker now left with black lips, black lungs, black gums,

Where's the life wished for?

It's four in the morning walking by the shore,

Calm from out but inside there's a loud roar,

Asking for no more,

Worn out feels like a long-lasting war,

Blood and gore,

Blood on the floor, blood on the walls and door,
Feeling sore as all the tears poured down,
Looking around, there's a little frown,
Depressed drowning through what life had to offer.

– Salmeen Al Hathrash

NEVER REALISED

Lifting weight with all of the hate,
All of the thoughts straight mess in my head,
Trying to move on, but hold on wait,
What was it that you told me?
Hmm, you'll never let me fade,
Now I'm lost in your thought,
How could it be, that's what I'm thinking about,
I never realised I wasn't important,
Never realised I was kicked out,
Nor did I realise who was I to fight for,
Let that be I Never knew I was at war.

– Salmeen Al Hathrash

SUGAR AND SWEET

They turned their backs,

You were lost, off your tracks,

You try to find your way, your path,

You find solace in being by yourself,

You choose isolation,

You sit alone, none with you,

You find life to be true, crazy,

You look at them not with hopes,

But just to smile and think how you messed up,

You had your cup filled when you shouldn't,

But now you know not everything sugar and sweet is good,

Sometimes your drink needs to be raw.

– Salmeen Al Hathrash

A PART TALE

The walk, the wish,
The love we frequently switch,
The moments, the Times,
Sitting thinking over it,
Lonely? Crazy isn't it Left alone,
Hoping life could get better someday,
Someway somehow just there,
Oh Lord this is how I pray,
Just one wish, I wish could stay,
Taking left instead of right,
Now you are left to yourself that's so bright,
Through the disaster the pain and crises,
You grew up with unwanted voices,
Nothing to decide no choices,
While it's just life and life it is,
Run running trying to get away from insanity,
That's how it's going to be.

– Salmeen Al Hathrash

THE REASON WHY HE KEPT GOING ON

Living up to someone's life,

There was never so much fun to see someone's smile,

All the sacrifices all the loss,

But he had his heart crossed,

Tried to stay even when it was tough,

Even when the path was rough,

There was always that one reason cause of which he kept holding on,

That at moments of hardship she was the one who kept him strong.

– Salmeen Al Hathrash

HOPELESS LOVE

This love is hopeless,
Stayed and messed,
Tried to love the fullest.
We are getting aggressive,
Fighting over unwanted choices,
Where have I lost you,
Tell me if my love was due,
Give me a hint, leave me a clue,
There was affection though,
But where was it lost who knows,
Now there are just pictures and memories,
Memories where I feel hurt and smile too,
This is life I can't move on, what to do?
You are on my mind,
And I wanted you to know.

– Salmeen Al Hathrash

DEAD WITH EMOTIONS.

There are feelings and emotions we don't show,
Seems like cold dead inside,
Give me paper and pen,
I'll pour everything out,
Emotions you won't even know what it's about,
There's a lot of life that we hide,
There is not much they know,
Cry to alone smile with none,
The emotion is different not many understand,
Everyone has their own.

– Salmeen Al Hathrash

LOST IN THE MIST OF THOUGHTS

Feeling some kind of a way,

There is a lot to say,

I feel some kind of a way,

Hold what could I be doing wrong,

Why do I feel weak?

Give me power why can't I feel strong,

They tell things would be alright,

staying up all night,

Trying to hold on tight,

Waiting for the right time,

waiting wasting seems like I'm doing a crime,

Line after line after the other another line,

With all these lines I've lost my smile,

All I did was rhyme, rhyme, rhyme,

While I lost the shine,

Trying to run of to the woods,

Get away from all this pain,

All the energy gone in vain,

such a shame,

Trying to figure out life,

standing on a hill thinking on top of a mountain,

trying to pay the bill thinking I got everything,

where have I got lost.

SWEET AND SOUR

Life is a mess,

When to smile when to be stressed,

The harder we try to look away,

The faster we fall prey,

Trying to smile in the most of pain,

We find solace in smokes and drinks,

World wouldn't have been this sour,

If we knew how much sugar to pour,

We complain about things harsh we have its checklist,

When there's a chance for sweetness, we say sorry diabetics.

– Salmeen Al Hathrash

A NEW CHANGE

Meet new people have a smile,
Think out of the box,
Why stand at the roadside,
When you got to cross.
Life is short live it all,
Why do you worry when you got to make the call?
Scared of heights or the lonely nights,
Or are you scared that you may fall,
Put the fear away,
Take a part in the play,
It may not be your game but you sure will have a story to say.

– Salmeen Al Hathrash

RUSTED IRON

Iron with rust, wounds still fresh,
Dreaming of stars while still on earth,
Isn't it stupid thoughts so messed,
Trying to reach far,
No idea what we come for,
Life is short we are still setting bars,
Isn't it stupid what we think about,
Forgetting the importance, the mains left out.

– Salmeen Al Hathrash

LOST IN THE MIST OF LIFE

She was lost, Indecisive needed support,
Trying hard to sort things out,
But at what cost,
She never realised.
She put up with a lot,
Ups and downs never ending mess in her life,
She just went on never complained,
The world never realised cause she always had a smile.
People walked in and out,
Imagining how things could be better,
She never thought how things could get about,
At times she just gave up and left it for later,
Walked with the flow of life which she was offered.

– Salmeen Hathrash

TOXIC RELATIONSHIP

Standing here staring at a wall,

Wondering, what was the point of this all?

Thinking was I asked to put in this much effort?

All I wanted was it to work where did I go wrong? How did I fall?

Wrong calls.

Heart and soul all in,

Realised was taken for granted,

Came crashing in,

I did it the way you asked me to,

Then you ask me to,

And then act out what am I to do?

Call me stupid call me fool.

Losing faith losing hope,

Losing myself too,

With all this drama I can't cope,

My mistake was loving you.

Toxic like I willingly jumped in a poisoning pool,

Still standing in front of a wall,

Wondering, how did I even love you.

– Salmeen Hathrash

PALACE OR A CASTLE

My minds a palace,

Trying to get my mind at peace,

By myself at the streets, weeks after weeks all that I believed my stress has increased,

Mind in a castle, finding solace, all my pain is it valid? Is This what you call madness,

War cries, taking long strides,

Came crashing down in seconds so few,

Where's the pride,

The fall the rise, and all your lies that came as surprise,

Wasn't a surprise cause you gave all the signs to what was on the line,

Won't say I wasted my time, lesson learned, and I'll remember it through my life.

– Salmeen Hathrash

BALANCE?

Palace in my mind,
Minds a palace,
In search of the light,
The light which brings balance,
Balance which I need in life,
Life in which I need silence,
All we speak of is magic,
Magic like all we do is hope,
Hoping life gets a little less dramatic,
Traumatic life through time getting chocked.

– Salmeen Hathrash

UNCONSCIOUS DREAMS

We are lost,

With our thoughts we are losing ourselves more,

Got lot,

A lot of emotions God only knows where we could store,

Not our fault,

We thought life would be like waves hitting the shore,

Forgot the salt,

That comes with the sea like everything else we ignore,

Something we want,

Desires and fantasies all that we can't have, we adore,

Growing soft,

Softer and softer, our life's we got to reform.

FINDING SOLACE

I took my time,

I even went offline,

I don't know why I can't get you off of my mind,

I tried so hard to get you out of my life,

Your thoughts stick around I don't know why,

I knew you would never be mine,

I knew everything on the line,

I grew so attracted I don't know why,

Through the day through the night,

Your thoughts I hold on tight,

A year and more still stuck I don't why.

SHOULD I SOCIALISE?

Socialising with people
Thinking too much
Being judged
Afraid of their character
Haven't seen world much
Talk remove negativity
Speak what you feel to speak
Feel free
Never had any contact
Just two strangers who come across
What am I to say when I'm thinking too much?
Afraid of being misunderstood
Not knowing how you might take it
Lost in my thoughts cause I'm thinking too much
Maybe something might offend you
Maybe something might offend me
Trying to get on the same page

Pages apart cause I'm thing too much

I feel like there is still so much to see

To know that I end up worrying about what might happen

And if only I had gone through and said the things I wanted to say as such,

maybe things might be different, and I wouldn't end up thinking too much.

STILL WORRIED

Why am I worried? maybe I need to put an End to it,
Be me and not worry about being judged
Why was I even thinking too much?
Haven't slept in days,
Still stuck with thoughts,
Why won't this go away,
Why is it hard,
Is it a game you like to play?
Flashbacks of all the memories,
Trying to get through with this,
Still living with our short stories,
What is that I resist what is it that I miss,
Gave everything,
Now I'm holding on to nothing.

THROUGH THEIR GAMES.

It's a mind game they've been trying to play,

They've been telling you can't reach anywhere,

Losing your track lost in their words,

Felling hurt even when you know you can shake worlds,

Stressing out for no reason at all,

Walking to a cliff preparing for your own fall,

Toss a coin heads or tails,

Heads or tails doesn't matter don't put down your sail,

You've got lot to explore lot to see,

Don't let their maybes hold you like a tree,

Even trees grow and their roots flow,

Let their words be, what will speak? Your shine your glow,

Doors closed God will help you there,

You focus on what you got to achieve,

Loudmouth will try to shake your will,

Believe in yourself cause it's your reach,

Don't hold yourself back show them it's a fight and you're willing to kill.

UNTRUE DREAMS.

We are fighting through time,
Losing ourselves in the dark,
Hopes high everything will be alright,
Trying not to lose and get back on track,
In search of light, in search for answers,
Lot of questions a little confused,
Which ones are the opportunities which ones the chances?
Lot thoughts of darkness, we are consumed,
Trying to move trying to get over things,
Finding meaning,
Trying to fly trying to spread our wings,
Lost in life just happy while we are dreaming.

TALE IN A WRITER

Running around smiling thinking it's a beautiful day,
Writing, writing, writing,
They ask me what you have to say,
Going around running crazy,
One word cut, strike, think, think,
what could be better than this,
Wander in my thought,
They ask me today what you have got,
Hoping I could give them the best.
I'm hanging on to this writing thing,
Hoping I could get somewhere some way someday.
Some say I'm crazy I'm just wasting time,
Not getting anywhere,
After all the talks and when I've got nobody to talk to,
I sit by myself for a while,
Thinking what am I doing with my life,

Throwing all the moments away.

With the models, the builders and all the good-looking folks around me,

I'm just a writer a fighter within,

Bang, bang on my chest bang, bang in my head,

This is faith and this is how it's going to be.

Don't ask me what I'm going to do,

You need not bother,

I've got in this alone,

It's not going to change anytime soon,

I'm hanging on to this writing thing,

Hoping I could get somewhere some way someday

Repeating the same shit,

This is my game, and this is how I play.

-

A LITTLE HAPPIER

As the curtains fall
It's back to what no one realises
Little things that penalises
And no one to go to
Just empty halls
We all do know
Things come
Things go
Can't we hold back?
The things that flow
Flow so flow
In way it has to glow
Let the world know
The little things we hide
And don't really show
Why is it so
Why is it so

Is it just with me?

Or are there people too

People who suffer

And want to be free

Can't it be easy

Can't it be a little happier narrative story.

BELIEVE, DON'T YOU WORRY

It's not the end of the world
It's just part of the moment
Good times don't come to a halt
It's all set
You know it's not going to last
Don't you think of the past
Let the world know
You are coming fast
When the hard times come by
Don't you worry
Believe, don't you go crazy
You've got time
A walk a talk
Don't you fear the dark
Don't you run
Bad moments come

A little so we can have fun
Bad moments come
Don't you look back
Don't you turn
Bad moments come
Keep walking ahead.

LITTLE WORDS LITTLE THINGS

I put my hand on my heart and scream out loud,
Oh girl, this is not what I wish for
I'm lost
And without you I'm just a corpse
In a shroud all wrapped and all out
A corpse that started a war
To get the glance of the view through the shore,
Of what they call the beausty
I fell for
And kept on wishing for a little more than just more
I'd bring the moon the stars
The sun the clouds
Just for you
Find you in a crowd
With my eyes closed
And the last thing I'd loved to do

Hold on to you
Keep bleeding out
Just to save what I love that's what it's all about
The cute little things you do
Got me going all through
Be the one to guard you at night
Be the one you could hold on tight to
This is a little I could do
Just to have you
Hold on have you
Trust me I need you
Not a poet nor is this a poem
Just little words
Just to get you smile
Cause I am all about you.

FREE OUT

Feel the bird, locked in a cage
Freedom taken away
Somethings hurt, somethings are strange
But some risks are worth the pay.
Set the bird free
Open the cage let it go
See listen to the beautiful humming
That it will have for you
Smile let your mind free
Forget it
And then see
Theres more to this world.

BREAK

Taking flights
Flying through clouds through the sky
Getting away from pain
A break needed
Get away from the world
Yea isolated
Let them not know you exist
Poof gone for a time
I have the strength to fix it
Swing hit
Aaah leave it
Instead Meditate
Till I feel right to levitate
And get off my head and hit straight
For now, it's back to bed
Till I land this flight of life great.

LOST IT

I start to lose hope
Start to lose faith
The monster within starts to get loose
This the life I was not to choose
I let you in
I let you close
Theres nothing left
How much more can I lose
Let me win let me win
Cause there is a lot to begin
I'm a little lost a little confused
A lot harmed and more than just abused
I got ripped apart
Ripped of my heart
Your method truly an art
I din know where to start
But now it's time to depart.

WE MOVE ON

We fall we rise
We rise to stand tall
We stand tall for a better call
We call on a better choice
We take a choice to become wise
We are wise when we take the shot
We take shots to learn a lot
We learn a lot by the mistake we make
Mistakes are made by every human
So don't you hide
Hiding is for cowards
We are strong we stay in the fight
We hold and move forward
We move on
We stay in not looking for light
But instead making it
Brighter than bright

Stronger than strong

Cause mistakes are mistakes

But it isn't wrong

But it is if you don't stake it all

All on the line

So, move on.

CREATE HISTORY

Leave back a legacy
Let them remember you for centuries
Make a name create history
Let them know it wasn't easy
Let them know your name
Leave back your fame
Fight like a warrior
Live like a survivor
Let them know you were a fighter
Went through all
Make them feel like the tightest situation was lightest
The hardest was easiest.

WOULD YOU MIND

Would you mind
If spoke what I felt like
Would you mind
If I waited and tried
Hold on I'm slipping away
Up all night trying on
Hope you don't mind
I'm here making all the bad choices
This world of mine
Crisis
I thought it would go on to be easy
Easy to me
Would you mind
Holding on to me
Not letting go.

MAKE IT HAPPEN

I will make it through
Make it happen
With the morning dew
Make a move
I realise I got moves but few
Still make it happen.
Step by step move on
March forward in the dust
Keep on till all the dust is gone
Not to look back cause I'm moving ahead
The path is set I'm moving straight
I'll make it through
Make it happen
Make it through hard times
Make it through all the rise and falls
The pain the wounds and scars
This is a war

A war in my mind
I'll make it through
Make it happen
Going on all night
Fight against the mind
It's time to shine
I'm making it through
Give me the time
I'll make it happen.

ALL I WANTED

lost in a world so real, the world so cruel
all these emotions wanting to feel
along the path there was lot to tell
I chose to keep silent, as the pain was insane
kept on, kept going.
all I wanted was to look out in the sky
flow my thoughts with the clouds
write, write, write on
all I wanted was feelings I lost over time
thoughts that used play in my mind
all I wanted was to glow a little brighter
have someone to hold a little tighter
all I wanted was to
stay strong a smile a little wider.

TOUGH TIMES

No matter about the dark
Theres always the light
Don't hold me back
Cause I've been up all night
I got a long way to go
Losing myself
Walking this path all alone
Show me the way, hold my hand
Cause I am not giving up
Not far away is a place I call home
Eeey sup?
What have you been through?
It was pretty much but I stood tough.
There was a time I dropped wept and hoped it was the end
Wept for so long I had to take a stand wipe off dust off and walk on
Tough maybe the moment tougher you are to send it off.

LET THEM

It's easy when we speak about someone
It's easy blaming someone
Thinking things by time will be gone
Doing all of that yeah it felt fun
But never realised how it stung that someone
Never bothered never felt
Never thought how they dealt
Stop pointing
Stop accusing
Do appreciate
Do encourage
Let them smile for something you do
Let them smile for them being part of you.

LET IT GO, BE YOU

Life does hit hard you do fall down, fight it back with all you got

While the time flies and you smile don't you get caught

We all know there's a world across that line, but it's got cost of pain and misery

A story one with a smile a frown a jump and a fall

Let it not end with stepping back take a stand make a call

Life will punch kick and laugh, fighting back? people will call you crazy, maybe

Don't let it go don't let it be, don't you see it's your win name it victory

Close your eyes goo blank hold your breath meditate

See what you feel in that darkness brings you to what you levitate

Stress it out, think it straight at the end of the day life's torture is just a thought locked in the head

Set it free let it go, be you.

SET ME FREE

I don't have many words I know not much,
I speak very little, know not what I thought,
My minds a mess, Lord knows what it is,
Set me free, set me free let this world see me be.
Little I am little I know to think,
Little I am little to fight,
Teach me, teach me, I want myself to be set free.
Let me be, let me free, let the world see that I'm not anyone else but me.
I want to be myself don't force me to change,
A different me makes me feel pretty strange,
Don't stare if you really care
Let me be me, help me be better than what I was yesterday,
Let me be, set me free, set me free.

THIS IS LOVE

Every time she smiles my world shines
Every time she hides away my world runs in search for those eyes
Theres a lot to speak a lot to say
But it's she all over my mind

Bright blue skies, bright beautiful eyes.
Got me going through time.
I'm down and gone cause of that beautiful smile.
Theres a lot to love in the ocean it's worth the dive.
Her eyes hold the universe it's worth the try.

Shut my eyes think of her cuddle the pillow
All night long
This is love isn't nothing wrong
Every chance of a glance
This heart wants to dance

Lost in thoughts where she is mine

Smiling the world thinks I'm crazy

Thinking of her all night long

This is love isn't nothing wrong.

-

SHE IS ALL

A pretty girl came along bringing the shine
Brighten up my life
She smiled flicked her hair
No don't care oh God I couldn't stop
Stay there keep stare
I told her I love you woke up to a dream
Every night cuddles the pillow she'll be mine one day for sure
Here there my minds running everywhere
She is pretty
How pretty? Let me share
Her face makes my heart chase the steps
Her eyes shine the universe
Her smile makes everything else look cheap

SHE LOVED, NOW SHE HOPES

Month after month

Kept loving a lot

She had it in for him

She looked for the heroes in a devil

She failed she tried kept hanging on

Months after months

Holding on trying to stay strong

While all along she failed to realise the person, she was with turned wrong

Had not a single feel never really bothered

Her world came crashing down

Never was the same for her

Now she sits under the dark skies

Wishing on stars

Hoping the world will realise

Hoping she'd once again smile

All night wide awake she's left with the scars he left

EMOTIONS TOOK A LIFE BUT BOUGHT A SMILE

"All this emotion killing me
All the reality that I hide
What do you know about?
Things aren't that easy
You see me smiling it's just a thought
Theres a million tears I hide
My heart wants to pump hard
I hold it on keep it silent
I want to shed all the tears, sit all day and cry
Let it all out, cry out loud.
Scream to the top of my voice
Scream and shout…"
These were his thoughts his last words
As he screamed in himself one last time
As he looked at himself before taking his last breaths
As the tears dropped and he choked through the ceiling his soul departed with a smile on his face

CAN I NOT

Can I never be the same again?
Can I never get rid of this pain?
Can I never get you out of my brain?
Don't I have the right to feel sane,

Shame on me for letting you in,
Blame all on me for letting you go,
Steam it off in my membrane,
Scream it off laying on the cold floor,

Did you even care, why did I even dare,
Was it even fare for you to leave without a farewell,
Hell.
Why did I even bother to be there?

LOOK IN

Dream on fear not
Fear never of what you think
It's just a thought
We have what we need, let it sink in.
Believe in what you could do
Believe in yourself
Believe in what you could be
Who knows what you could show?
Learn to love
Learn to live
It's your life
Don't look around look in.

IT'S JUST A WORD

Love is a word, less a feeling, It's a game they are just playing,

Tell me not of those emotions,

There's more to that short sensation

IT'S MEANT TO BE.

This is What it's Meant to Be
I've been thinking about it all Day
I love you in everyway
I've got trust issues she said
It's alright it's okay
I don't mind
Its life and I am not scared
This how it is, and I am not afraid
I put my faith in you
Now its fading away,
This is love, a game for two
But I can't play
Play all by myself
This is making me crazy
I don't want to lose myself all again
It's hard for me
Let's see or maybe

This is what it's meant to be
Life is cruel
Sometimes this world too
But what can we do?
It's been a long time
It really has been a while
Getting myself together
Piece by piece
It was hard solving my puzzle
Now I need a wall
Long tall build across me

DEPRESSED?

Depressed?

Thinking you can make it through the night?

There's a lot to thoughts and questions,

There's a lot to the fights you fought,

There's a lot to, to those hard heart held situations.

Want to cry?

Look through the sky,

Through space and time,

Look away and look closely who knows what you realise.

It's easy to speak up,

When you know what it is about.

GOING ON

I've been going on,

Trying to move on,

Thinking it was easy,

Thinking I was strong.

I'm lost trying to find my path,

Lost every step getting harder and hard,

Where am I going, I know not?

But now it's just a start.

Are you mad or crazy?

I come across this all the time,

MISTAKES GRUDGES HATE

Mistakes grudges hate,

Living it through being my own bait,

Pain was my energy all this while,

Risk was it risk was me,

Dug my hole did not realise,

Where am I to look,

Where am I to search,

Mistakes I have made,

Hanged my life by the hook,

Haven't done anything great.

All this grudge I kept to myself,

Hadn't had enough,

They asked me to look away,

But all I did was look in,

Look it through.

What's the hate for,

Why am I fighting this war?

When I know I lost it all,
Never knew till I had my fall,
I lost it by the night,
I took time to know I wasn't right.
I made mistakes,
I hid my grudges,
Ended with hate.

LOCKED UP.

Maybe I'm crazy maybe I'm not,

Maybe they've spoken things I don't know about,

Maybe I'm getting through this,

Someone come get me out,

I've lost everything I've got

Don't know about my route

Maybe I live in doubt,

Stuck in a crowd,

Maybe I want to scream loud,

Maybe they can't hear me shout,

No words coming out my mouth,

A nightmare

Maybe I'm locked in a haunted house,

THIS IS WHAT IT IS

Life has given me a lot
Taken a lot
I don't know what to be talking about
I try to smile through the day
Hoping it to be better than yesterday
Where is the power within me?
A little time a break seriously
Cause the times been long
Things being wrong
Trying to be strong
The conscious within wants to be free
God knows when it would be

THAT ONE SMILE

There was pain,

He walked alone all he had was his shadow,

Thinking he could make through,

He kept trying kept falling,

There were things he kept regretting,

The pain he had enough,

He became hollow no feeling no emotions,

He kept going,

Going on, on a path that led nowhere,

Almost done fed up with life,

He kept pushing God gave him a reason to push forward,

A rainy day, as the rain poured,

There he kept looking on,

Someone so beautiful walked in and changed the phase of his life,

There were still ups and downs and he kept holding on,

Time passed he felt hard but never gave up,
Who knew one day eventually he would have her,
He never saw someone so pretty,
Never so cute,
Lost in that smile,
And finding his world in that universe filled eyes,
Love set aside,
Life left behind,
Struggles forgotten,
There he had a reason
He kept pushing kept moving on,
Cause that smile had changed his life.

WALK IN WALK OUT

Lot to choose from, Lot of choices,

Never thought never realised,

Walked a path unknown,

Am I crazy out of my mind,

Trying to make my way,

Way out of everything that comes through,

Hard to explain hard to say, what is this what's going on?

Life is simple.

You walk in, live it, walk out,

Don't confuse with what's life about,

I've lived it, it's time to walk out,

Last words that flipped in his head before he dropped down floors after floors crashing down in his thoughts,

HOPE AND MOVE

Walking through the streets crossing houses and peoples,

Trying to divert your thought,

Finding a place to get away from all the evils in your mind,

Finding someone to talk it out,

Losing your patience,

Losing what could be all,

Losing all the time you got,

You were standing tall now you are on the urge to fall,

You were smiling living,

Now slowly you die out,

Finding the person you loved,

Leaning against the wall there isn't any more time left,

Self-harm cuts and scratches,

Punching the walls, the door,

You are going places,

Now you've gone too far,

Fight the demon, fight the monster,

You may not win, but you shouldn't lose either,

Take a step ahead, don't look back,

Sort it in your head, you got to run fast get back on track,

You may seem crazy, might have lost the will to live,

You got to chill,

You fall to get back up.

TAKE ME BACK HOME

Take me back home,

Take me back to that place I never felt alone,

Take me back home,

Take me back where every day I see my mom,

Take me back home,

Where I never have to wait for Dad to phone,

Take me back home,

To my siblings with whom I've grown,

Take me back to where I was born,

Take me back home.

BY MY OWN

I'm getting over you, I'm getting over us,
Not really sure but, you were dangerous,
You played me over bad, I never realised,
It took me time to stand on my feet,
By that time, I had actually turned very weak,
Now I'm moving on, but not so strong,
Going to walk this path this time just by my own

•

TALE OF LIFE

It's easy to judge easy to blame,
Easy to call liar as a name,
You won't know the sufferings nor the pain,
You haven't been riding the same train,
Fuel his emotions fuel the rage,
You haven't been the one locked in a cage,
Never understood nor have you thought,
The poor person was going through a lot,
Tried to take his life tried it all,
But he was too scared to take the fall,
Now he is sitting there trying to recall,
The moments the memories,
Looking in the sky wishing if they could've understood him well,
This is a small story I got to tell,
Suffered throughout life,
With cries and smiles,

Risked his voice kept it quiet,

Never complained never mentioned,

But always thought this life wasn't his meant.

BY THE TIME

What happens when we all fall down?
And the time isn't right,
You got no strength can't pull yourself up,
You try to be strong,
Think it's bright even without light,
You drink by the bottle even when you've got cups.
You look through hoping for the right time,
Hoping you'll be fine,
But got nothing left to say,
You know it will take you a while,
But you say never mind,
Life is a game you ready to play.

IT IS YOUR LIFE

There's love, there is hate,

There're sweet moments,

Then there are moments when you were just a bait,

This is how life is,

You got to get it straight,

All you want to make is one wish,

That you could get all the hate out of your head,

Just live it, smile through it,

You know at the end of the day it is you, your thought and the bed,

No one is going to be by your side,

No one is going to be part of your life,

No one is the reason for your smile,

No one is part of why you cry,

Get ahead get your life right,

At the end of the night, it was always you by yourself and no one playing in the line.

Be who you are, be what makes you laugh a little longer, cry a little shorter and smile a little wider,

This is your right, and no one can take it away,

It is your game, and you choose how you want to play,

Never look back, never lose track, or you'll never make it.

A SHORT TALE

With every love story comes heart breaks,
Empty pockets and empty bucket list checks,
Walking down the path kicking stones in your way,
Looking down as you walk not knowing what to say,
Stare through the sky counting stars,
Taking deep breaths trying to get somewhere far,
Cutting relations as people speak,
Your mind is tensed temper at its peak,
You are taking steps never you thought you would,
Thinking what this world is about,
Am I mad thinking this life I could,
Could I make it?

LEARN

For all the good and bad times,

For all the frowns and the smiles,

For all the lows and highs,

There was always somewhere in between you were stuck,

Trying to find your way, trying to look around,

Hoping what's going on isn't wrong,

You halt and turn look back, in fear and thoughts,

Do I still have time, what is this about?

But you were crazy enough to go along,

So don't sit and complain on,

Cause every language is different,

Hard to understand, but why not just smile and learn.

LOST IN WORDS

There are things I wish to say,
Things I wished you'd know,
Can't find the words to express,
By the time I find my words I lose my way,
Let it drown down slow,
Panic attack lot buttons which one to press.
I'm lost now trying to be found,
Every time Someone tries, I lose myself more,
What is this sorcery?
They tell me get a drink this is the only cure,
I insist on standing tall fight fall try again I'll win I'm pretty sure.

A MISTAKE

Thoughts of thoughts getting me to think,

Life was simple and plain but then you walked in,

Filled with joy and happiness,

I climbed hills and mountains,

Just to know I was climbing to my own downfall with all the strain and pain,

Every time I get up dust off someone comes by pushing me down,

Now I lay in this cold sand expecting a warm hand,

That would take me away from this cold world,

That would hold on never let go,

As I think of this, I'm taking off slow,

Emotions are dead no more smile on my face,

It's my mistake let them get the best of me.

GETTING BACK

The beach side the wind breeze,
The stars shine with the moonlight,
Every broken heart story.
Trying to find the truth in the skies,
Through the dark clouds finding life,
Trying to find out the hidden lie.
Been there through it,
Was it worth it was it perfect,
Even with experience this soft heart blew it.
Back to the sand the sea the moonlight and the stars that shine the night,
Hoping to get back, one more chance hoping to get right,
Hoping to get back.

SOMETIMES I JUST WISH

Sometimes I cry sometimes I weep,

Sometimes I wish to see what is deep,

Sometimes there's a lot I wish to speak,

But I keep it to myself,

Sometimes I wish to live,

Sometimes I just wish to walk off,

But that sometimes is yet to come.

www.ingramcontent.com/pod-product-compliance
Lightning Source LLC
LaVergne TN
LVHW091103150826
845673LV00002B/704

* 9 7 9 8 8 8 7 0 4 3 2 6 5 *